LIFE IN BRITAIN

BRITAIN in TUDOR TIMES

Fiona Macdonald

W
FRANKLIN WATTS
LONDON•SYDNEY

© 2003 Franklin Watts

First published in 2003 by
Franklin Watts
96 Leonard Street
London
EC2A 4XD

Franklin Watts Australia
45-51 Huntley Street
Alexandria
NSW 2015

ISBN: 0 7496 4871 6

A CIP catalogue record for this book is available from the British Library

Printed in Malaysia
Planning and production by Discovery Books Limited
Editor: Helen Dwyer
Design: Keith Williams
Picture Research: Rachel Tisdale

Photographs:
cover, title page, border & 8 Bridgeman Art Library, small cover image and border
Stuart Carter, 4 Bridgeman Art Library/Bibliotheque Centrale, Ghent, 5 Discovery
Picture Library/Alex Ramsay, 6 & 7 top Bridgeman Art Library, 7 bottom Mary Evans
Picture Library, 9 top Bridgeman Art Library, 10 Mary Evans Picture Library, 11 top
Mary Rose Trust, 11 bottom Weald and Downland Open Air Museum, 12 Mary
Rose Trust, 13 top Alex Ramsay, 13 bottom Mary Rose Trust, 14 Mary Evans Picture
Library, 15 top Alex Ramsay, 15 bottom Mary Rose Trust, 16 Discovery Picture
Library/Alex Ramsay, 17 top Bridgeman Art Library, 17 bottom Alex Ramsay, 18
Bridgeman Art Library, 19 top Bridgeman Art Library/Asprey & Co., London, 19
bottom Mary Rose Trust, 20 & 21 top Bridgeman Art Library, 21 bottom
Shakespeare's Globe Picture Library/John Tramper, 22 & 23 top Discovery Picture
Library/Alex Ramsay, 23 bottom & 24 Bridgeman Art Library, 25 top Mary Evans
Picture Library, 25 bottom Discovery Picture Library/Alex Ramsay, 26 English
Heritage/Nigel Corrie, 27 top Mary Evans Picture Library, 27 bottom Discovery
Picture Library/Alex Ramsay, 28 British Library, 29 top Discovery Picture
Library/Alex Ramsay, 29 bottom Mary Rose Trust

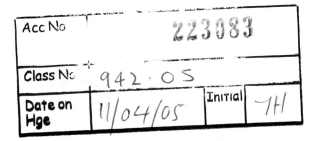

BRITAIN in TUDOR TIMES

Contents

About the Tudors

The Tudor age lasted for just over a century, from 1485 to 1603. It is named after a powerful royal family called the Tudors.

The Tudors had to fight to win power. From 1455 to 1485, there were civil wars in England between rival **nobles**. Bandit gangs and private armies terrorised people in many parts of the country.

Henry Tudor – the son of a Welsh lord and an English noblewoman – fought against King Richard III, and defeated him. Henry became King Henry VII of England and Wales, and Lord of Ireland. (Scotland was an independent country in Tudor times, with its own king and queen, government and laws.) Henry was a harsh ruler, but he brought peace.

Compared with today, there were few people then in Britain – only around 4 million at the start of the Tudor age. By 1603, there were around 6 million. That is around one-tenth of the total today. Most Tudor people lived in the countryside and made their living from the land.

▲ Knights in armour fighting at the Battle of Barnet, 1471. This was one of many bloody battles during the civil wars that lasted from 1455 to 1485, and are known as the Wars of the Roses. The last Wars of the Roses battle was in 1485, at Bosworth Field, when Henry Tudor defeated King Richard III.

▲ Hardwick Hall, in Derbyshire, is one of the most stylish Tudor stately homes. It was built between 1590 and 1597 for a rich and powerful noblewoman, Elizabeth, Countess of Shrewsbury. Her initials 'E. S.' can still be seen at the top of the towers.

Major towns

Major ports

Major religious and cultural centres

Newcastle-upon-Tyne

York

Hull

Great Yarmouth

Boston

King's Lynn

Norwich

EAST ANGLIA

Cambridge

Ipswich

COTSWOLDS

Oxford

Swansea

London

Bristol

Southampton

▲ This map shows the most important British cities and ports around 1550. In Tudor times, like today, most British people lived in the south-east of England. In the early 16th century, the richest areas were the cloth-making districts of East Anglia and the Cotswolds. By the end of the century, the area around London was more prosperous through expanding business and trade.

For many ordinary people, life was hard. Men and women did tough, physical work with no big machines to help them. There was no piped water, gas or electricity in their homes, and no bathrooms or showers. No medicines were available to help them fight common diseases, and people were often hungry.

In spite of this, the Tudor age was a time of great achievements. Tudor people built magnificent sailing ships, clever weapons and wonderful houses, designed amazing clothes, made daring voyages to distant lands, and developed many new styles of music and art.

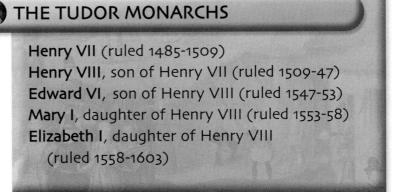

THE TUDOR MONARCHS

Henry VII (ruled 1485-1509)
Henry VIII, son of Henry VII (ruled 1509-47)
Edward VI, son of Henry VIII (ruled 1547-53)
Mary I, daughter of Henry VIII (ruled 1553-58)
Elizabeth I, daughter of Henry VIII
   (ruled 1558-1603)

Tudor People

Tudor people were divided into two main groups. There were a few nobles (rich landowners with titles) but most people were commoners (ordinary people with no power). These two groups lived very different lives.

Nobles were rich because they owned most of the land. They were also well educated, and had servants to look after them. Nobles demanded respect and obedience from ordinary men and women. Many nobles were friends of the Tudor kings and queens. They were given top jobs in the royal government and were often also members of **Parliament** (the national law-making assembly). Some nobles fought as army commanders. Others served as judges, keeping law and order in their local communities.

Ordinary lives

Most commoners were poor and powerless. They owned no land, except perhaps a garden plot, and had few personal possessions. They did hard, exhausting, physical work and most had little chance of improving their lives.

◄ In this engraving (printed picture) from the time, Queen Elizabeth I is sitting on a very grand throne, listening to a meeting of Parliament. Noblemen, bishops and judges sit on padded benches in front of her. The four men kneeling on the floor in the centre of the picture are busily writing down records of the speeches.

A few commoners were more fortunate. Top merchants and craftworkers who lived in towns grew rich through trade. They became town councillors or mayors. There were also a few wealthy farmers, called **yeomen**, who owned large farms that produced valuable grain and animals to sell.

Loyalty and the law

Nobles and commoners all owed loyalty to the Tudor kings and queens. They also had to obey the law. Death was the punishment for many crimes, even for stealing a sheep. New laws and taxes were suggested by the king or queen and their advisors, but they had to be approved by Parliament. There were serious quarrels when monarchs and Parliaments could not agree.

▼ This Tudor picture shows condemned men in the stocks (a wooden frame that fitted round their hands and feet). Thieves, cheats and liars might all be punished in this way. Passers-by could shout insults at the criminals, or throw mud and rotten food at them.

▲ Housewives and women servants wash clothes and spread them out on grassy river-banks to dry and bleach (get whiter) in the sun. Washing was very hard work. Tudor women had no piped hot water or washing and drying machines to help them. This painting on vellum (calf skin) is now in the British Library in London.

Exploring the world

In the Tudor period, for the very first time, people in Britain made contact with distant countries. Explorers sailing to the Americas, western Africa, and southern and eastern Asia brought back reports of peoples they had seen there. Sailors from all round the world found work on European ships, and visited British ports. Some, including probably the first black people to settle in Britain, decided to stay.

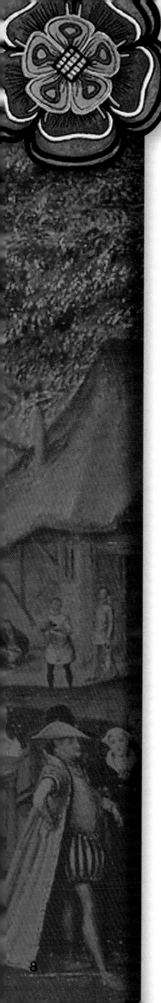

Families and Communities

Belonging to a family was an advantage in Tudor times. Family members helped and cared for one another. Some also worked together in family businesses or farms.

People relied on their local community for help. Friends and neighbours shared food, loaned tools, cared for each other's children and worked together to harvest corn and shear sheep.

Getting married

In rich or noble families, marriages were usually arranged. Parents chose marriage partners for their children to unite with other rich families or to help business deals. Rich children were often married very young. By law, girls could marry at 12 and boys at 14.

▼ Members of the local community at Bermondsey (then a village close to London) enjoy themselves at a celebration in 1570. Today, this splendid painting can be seen at Hatfield House, a stately home in Hertfordshire.

Young commoners had more freedom to choose their own husbands or wives, and most did not marry until they were at least 25. When they reached their teens, they went to work in nobles' houses, craft workshops or on farms. They lived with their employers until they had saved up enough money to rent a house and buy furniture. Then they got married and moved into their own homes.

From the cradle to the grave

Women from rich or noble families often had ten babies, or more. Mothers in ordinary families only had four or five. Probably half of all children died before they were five. If a Tudor boy or girl managed to survive to adulthood, they would be lucky to reach 50 years of age.

▲ This cloth, made to decorate an altar in a church, is embroidered with portraits of Catherine Neville, the noblewoman who paid for it, and her thirteen daughters. They are all shown kneeling, in prayer. This beautiful piece of needlework is kept in the Victoria & Albert Museum in London.

'STURDY BEGGARS'

Many communities faced serious problems when large numbers of poor, homeless, unemployed people – travelling in family groups or gangs – arrived in villages and small towns, begging for food and shelter. Sometimes they threatened violence if they did not receive help. Tudor governments passed laws limiting the amount of food or money that could be given to beggars. They also ordered that all 'sturdy' (fit and healthy) beggars should be made to work.

▼ Wandering beggars who refused to work, or who used violence to demand money, were whipped out of towns and villages – as shown in this woodcut from the time.

Country Life

Ordinary country people worked on farms belonging to nobles or yeomen, or else as servants in their big, comfortable homes. Some earned daily wages. Others were 'paid' with free food and lodgings.

Men did jobs such as ploughing, digging ditches, harvesting, cutting hay, and caring for sheep and cattle. They also worked as builders, **thatchers,** and general labourers. Women were cooks, cleaners, dairy-workers, laundresses, children's nurses and ladies' maids. They spun thread, sewed clothes and weeded crops growing in the fields.

Cottage life

Country people usually lived in tiny cottages which they rented from nobles or yeomen. For food they grew vegetables in their gardens, and kept chickens and a pig. In rocky areas, the cottages were mostly built of stone. Elsewhere, they were constructed of a timber frame filled in with lath (small strips of wood) and plaster. These homes were small, dark and cramped. Most had only one or two rooms. There was no running water and no bathroom, just an earth pit used as a lavatory in the yard. Very few people had glass in their windows. To keep out the wind and rain, they covered the windows with wooden shutters or oiled cloth.

◄ This woodcut shows Tudor labourers at work. The man at the front is sowing wheat seeds. The man at the back is guiding horses who are pulling a harrow – a farm tool with sharp spikes to break up lumps of earth, so that the wheat seeds will have smooth ground to grow in.

A carpenter's tool-kit found on board the wreck of the Tudor warship *Mary Rose*. Carpentry skills were essential, on land as well as at sea. Carpenters made all kinds of useful items from wood, such as furniture, doors and windows, carts, plates and drinking bowls.

'SHEEP EATING MEN'

Sheep-rearing, to produce wool to make cloth, was the most profitable farming in early Tudor times. From around 1450, many rich landowners put fences around the open grassland on their estates, and raised sheep there. This meant that ordinary people could no longer graze their own animals. Previously, each family might have kept a cow or a goat, to provide nourishing milk and cheese. Now they went hungry. Tudor people complained that 'sheep were eating men'.

Country crafts

Skilled craftworkers lived in villages and country towns, making useful goods to sell. Weavers wove cloth from wool and **flax**. Potters shaped clay into dishes and cooking pots. **Chandlers** melted beeswax and tallow (sheep's fat) for candles. Blacksmiths hammered iron into knives, tools, weapons and horseshoes. Cobblers and saddlers made leather buckets, shoes and harnesses for horses. Horses were used to travel long distances, and also to pull carts and heavy farm equipment such as ploughs.

A 16th-century yeoman farmer's house from the south of England, reconstructed at the Weald and Downland Open Air Museum, near Chichester in Sussex. It is built with a timber frame, lath-and-plaster walls, and a clay-tile roof.

Food and Famine

Most Tudor meals were not very healthy. If families were rich, they ate too much meat and fat and not enough fruit and vegetables. If they were poor, they sometimes had to survive on bread alone.

The best-fed Tudor people were yeomen farmers and their families. They raised their own animals for meat and milk, planted orchards for fruit and kitchen gardens for vegetables, and grew grain to make their own bread.

Tudor cooking

The main meal of the day was dinner, served at around 11 a.m. Breakfast was just a snack of bread, and supper was also a light, simple meal. Women from ordinary families cooked soups and stews of bacon, rabbit, vegetables and wild herbs in big iron pots over open fires. Bread was baked in brick ovens or on flat iron dishes.

Tudor people had no fridges or freezers. They preserved meat in tubs of salty water or by hanging it in smoky chimneys, and stored fruit and vegetables in cold attics and barns to eat in winter time. Rich families liked meat roasted on a spit – a metal stick that turned over an open fire. The meat was served with rich, spicy sauces. Sweet dishes were full of expensive luxuries like dried fruit, almonds, spices and sugar.

◄ An iron cooking pot, found on board the *Mary Rose*. It has legs so that it can stand in the hot ashes of a wood fire. For many Tudor families, pots like these were all they had for cooking hot meals.

During the Tudor era, many new foods from the Americas reached Britain for the first time, including potatoes, pineapples, chillies, sweet peppers and avocados.

The most common Tudor drink – for both adults and children – was very weak beer. It was safer than water from wells and streams, which was often polluted by human and animal waste. Country people also drank buttermilk and whey. These were left over when butter and cheese were made and were rather like thin yoghurt.

▲ The kitchen of a grand Tudor home – Burghley House, near Stamford in Lincolnshire. A large staff of cooks and servants worked here, cooking meals for the noble owners and their guests. In the background are the huge fireplace where meat was roasted on a spit, and the black iron door of an oven which was used to bake bread.

▼ Tudor plates, bowls, spoons, jugs and drinking flagons (big mugs). They are made from pottery, wood or pewter (a mixture of lead and tin). All were found in the wreck of the *Mary Rose*, but many fairly wealthy Tudor families, such as yeomen farmers, would have owned similar items.

The hungry years

As the population of Britain increased during the 16th century, there were many more people looking for work. Wages fell, food prices rose and the poorest people began to go hungry. Sometimes bad weather led to harvest failures, and there was not enough grain to make bread for everyone. Many people in northern and western Britain starved to death.

Towns and Trade

Most Tudor people did not live in towns. But they visited them often, travelling on horseback, in horse-drawn carts or, usually, on foot.

Country people went into the towns to consult a doctor or a lawyer, or to enjoy a seasonal fair – at midsummer, Christmas, or after harvest time. If they had the money, they might go to a theatre and watch a play.

Buying and selling

Most important of all, Tudor towns were centres of trade. The market was there, with stalls selling local farm produce, and many small shops and craft workshops (often part of a house). Traders also sold craft goods, especially cloth, produced in villages nearby. Some towns specialised in particular goods. Swansea sent thousands of tonnes of coal by sea to London; Great Yarmouth sent cod (caught off Iceland and Newfoundland) to markets in many parts of England. Expensive imported goods, such as silk from Italy or spices from Asia, were sold only in London or at the ports where they arrived.

▼ Women buying and selling fish in a town market around 1570. Most market traders were women. Country women travelled to towns on foot or on horseback to sell goods produced by their families.

Town houses

Most people lived in timber-framed houses infilled with lath-and-plaster or brick. Town houses were often tall and narrow to fit as many as possible into a street. Frequently they had a shop or showroom in the downstairs front room facing the street. Some had workshops at the back.

On the move

Ambitious young people moved to towns to find work or enrol as **apprentices**. They hoped to improve their chances of a secure, comfortable life by training for a well-paid career. When times were hard in the countryside, poor, hungry and unemployed people also flocked to the towns, hoping to get enough money – by begging or doing odd jobs – to buy food. They crowded together in run-down, old town buildings.

Poor relief

In some places there were so many poor and hungry people that town councils arranged special charity schemes, collecting taxes from rich citizens to give money to the poor. In the 1550s, the Tudor government passed laws setting up a national system of poor relief. Each local community had to make collections for its own poor.

▲ The front room of this Tudor house in Lavenham, Suffolk, was used as a shop. The windows had wooden shutters which were folded down to form a counter where goods for sale were displayed.

▼ Gold coins used during the reign of Tudor King Henry VIII and recovered from the wreck of the *Mary Rose*.

Grand Houses

Since around AD 1000, nobles in Britain had built strong castles to defend their lands. But, by Tudor times, new weapons such as cannon could smash through stonework and demolish walls.

Castles were no longer safe places to live – and they were damp and draughty. So rich Tudor families began to build grand new houses, to display their wealth and artistic taste.

Brick and glass

Large Tudor houses were often built of brick, or wood and plaster. Many had huge glass windows that let in light, warmth from the sun and fresh air. Outside, there were neat 'knot' gardens – beds of flowers laid out in complicated patterns, surrounded by tiny hedges of evergreen plants. People could relax in seats called arbours, which were surrounded by shady bushes or sweet-smelling plants.

Comfort and luxury

Big Tudor homes were designed as comfortable places to live. There were separate rooms for sleeping, cooking, dining in style and welcoming honoured guests.

◄ The recreated Tudor knot garden at Moseley Old Hall, in Cheshire. The neatly trimmed hedges have been laid out in complicated patterns, using a plant called box that stays green all year round.

The largest houses often had a huge upstairs room, known as a long gallery, where family portraits were displayed, and where women could walk and talk when the weather was too bad to go outdoors. Most rooms were lined with carved wood panelling, or with plaster moulded into patterns of fruit and flowers. Other walls were covered with thick **tapestries** – woven pictures that showed colourful hunting scenes or stories from myths and legends. Furniture, made from carved, polished wood, was big, heavy and comfortable. Chairs were padded with plump cushions, and beds were surrounded by cosy curtains made of embroidered wool.

▲ This magnificent bed, of carved wood, was made around 1570 for the noble family who lived in Gwydir Castle in north Wales. In Tudor times, it would have been hung with thick curtains on each side, to keep out the cold.

Centres of the community

These grand Tudor homes needed many skilled craftworkers to build them, and dozens of servants to run them. They were also the centres of many local communities. Ordinary people from nearby villages paid rent and taxes to the house-owner, and he had the power to punish them if they broke the law. Poor people waited outside the gates, to beg for money, food or warm clothes.

▼ Burghley House, near Stamford in Lincolnshire, is England's largest Tudor stately home. It was built for William Cecil, Queen Elizabeth I's most trusted advisor. It has large glass windows, and the walls are made of high quality local stone. They are topped with towers and elaborate carvings.

Clothes

All Tudor people wore clothes that were similar in shape. However, there were big differences between rich and poor in the materials used and how the clothes were decorated.

Women and girls dressed in heavy gowns with tight-fitting **bodices** and full, floor-length skirts. For comfort, they wore thin linen shifts (garments rather like nightdresses) underneath. They covered their hair with headscarves or close-fitting headdresses with trailing veils. Men and boys wore baggy shirts, usually topped by short **tunics** or jackets, and knee-length trousers. Priests, lawyers and some very old men wore long, loose robes.

Fashions for the rich

Rich Tudor men and women wore some of the most sumptuous clothes ever seen in Britain, made from silk and velvet, embroidered with gold and silver thread, and decorated with lace, fur and real jewels. They also liked to wear the latest fashions, copied from Spain and France. For women, these included low-cut necklines, long, stiffened bodices and padding around the hips. Fashions for men included padded shoulders and thighs, and also padded 'codpieces', which covered men's private parts.

► A fashionable young Englishwoman in early Tudor times, depicted by a famous German artist, Hans Holbein the Younger. Her gown has a tight-fitting bodice, and a long full skirt. She is wearing a close-fitting coif (cloth headdress) and a flowing, transparent veil. This picture is now in the Ashmolean Museum in Oxford.

In early Tudor times, rich men and women wore clothes decorated with hundreds of tiny cuts, to show off a different coloured fabric underneath. Towards the end of the Tudor era, huge ruffs (wide, wheel-shaped collars, made of stiffened linen and lace) were very popular.

Plain and simple

Ordinary people's clothes were made of coarse wool and rough, homespun linen, with few decorations. To keep warm, people wrapped themselves in long woollen cloaks, and wore knee-length, knitted woollen socks and flat leather boots or shoes. Very poor people went barefoot, or wore wooden clogs.

POMANDERS AND NOSEGAYS

Tudor people did not bathe very often. Even the richest homes did not have piped water supplies. But people believed that deadly diseases were caused by unpleasant smells. So they carried nosegays (posies of sweet-smelling herbs and flowers) or pomanders (decorated balls containing scented **resins**, herbs and spices). They believed that the sweet scents would drive away diseases.

▶ This pomander, crafted around 1580, was designed to hang from a necklace or belt, ready for its owner to smell at any time. It is made of silver-gilt (silver covered with real gold) and decorated with fine black enamel (a thin layer of jewel-like glass).

◀ Leather shoes, worn by Tudor soldiers, sailors and gentlemen, found on board the wreck of the *Mary Rose*. The shoes are flat, with broad toes, in typical Tudor fashion. They would have been worn with long, knitted socks or tight-fitting stockings sewn from thin woollen cloth.

Entertainment

Tudor people worked hard, but they also enjoyed themselves by listening to music, watching street performers such as acrobats and jugglers, going to the theatre, and playing many sports and games.

For ordinary people, fishing, wrestling and archery were favourite outdoor sports. Football was also very popular. All the men and boys in one village would get together in a huge team, to play against neighbouring villages or towns. Games were very rough, and lasted all day. There were no pitches. Players chased the ball through the streets and across the fields. People were often injured, and sometimes killed.

Rich men and women hunted deer on horseback, or used trained hawks to catch rabbits and small birds. Tudor people also liked entertainments that today we would consider very cruel, such as watching fights between two cockerels or between captive bears and trained dogs.

▼ This portrait of a group of wealthy card-players was painted by an unknown artist in the 1560s, possibly for a powerful noblewoman, the Countess of Warwick. Playing cards, invented in the Middle East, reached Britain around 1500, at the start of the Tudor age. They soon became so popular that laws had to be passed to stop cheating!

Sweet music

Travelling musicians played in streets and market places, or found work in noble families' great houses. There, they played gentle music on flutes, lutes and **viols**, or sang madrigals (songs with different parts for four or more people) while lords and ladies ate their meals. This was followed by the latest lively tunes for dancing. Tudor dances were very energetic, with lots of leaps, jumps, twists and twirls. Noble ladies also played a keyboard instrument called the virginals, which made a gentle, tinkling sound.

Plays and players

In towns and cities, Tudor people went to watch plays in newly built, round theatres. The well-off sat in covered seats on each side, while poorer people stood in the open space in front of the stage. They laughed at the actors' jokes, or booed and jeered if they did not like the play. In Tudor times only men were actors. Tudor people believed it was shocking for women to appear on stage. So teenage boys – in women's clothes, wigs and make-up – played all the female parts.

▲ A miniature (very small) painting showing Queen Elizabeth I holding a lute – a musical instrument with six strings which were plucked. Miniatures like this, with beautiful golden frames, were often pinned to clothes in the same way as jewellery. Today, this painting is at Berkeley Castle in Gloucestershire.

▶ The most famous Tudor playwright was William Shakespeare (1564-1616). Here his play, *The Tempest*, is being performed at a reconstructed Tudor theatre, the Globe, in London. The actors on stage are very close to the lively audience of 'groundlings' – ordinary people who stood to watch the latest plays.

Religious Quarrels

When the first Tudor, Henry VII, became king, religious life in Britain was run as it had been for centuries by the Roman Catholic Church. The leader of the Catholic Church was the Pope, and its headquarters were in Rome.

A few scholars – known as 'Reformers' or 'Protestants' – questioned Catholic teachings and complained that its priests were too interested in wealth and power. Most people, however, continued to remain Catholic.

▲ This is a rood-screen – a carved wooden screen that divided the holiest part of a church from the area where worshippers stood. It is beautifully decorated with delicate carvings and paintings of saints. Most rood-screens were destroyed by Protestants of the new Church of England. This one, at Attleborough in Norfolk, was hidden away, and survived.

Catholic churches

Catholic churches were decorated with statues, brightly painted walls, and stained-glass windows. There were gold crosses and candlesticks, and priests wore robes of red and purple silk. Church services included music, candlelight, **incense** and processions. All prayers, hymns and Bible readings were in **Latin**.

The need for an heir

Henry VIII, the second Tudor king, was a loyal Catholic. But his first wife had not produced a son and he wanted to get divorced and remarry. Divorce was not allowed by Catholic laws, unless the Pope gave special permission. When the Pope would not do this, Henry ordered the church in England to break away from Roman Catholic control.

◀ The ruins of Fountains Abbey in Yorkshire, closed by Henry VIII in 1539. Between 1536 and 1540, as part of his quarrel with the Pope in Rome, Henry VIII closed down all communities of monks and nuns in England, and gave their land and buildings to his loyal supporters.

In 1534, Henry VIII made himself Supreme Governor of the new English Church, and appointed priests he could trust to run it. Slowly, Protestant reforms were introduced.

▼ A portrait by a unknown English artist showing a mother and her baby, painted around 1595. The baby is dressed in fine robes, for its christening – a Christian ceremony in which a baby is given its first names, and its parents and godparents promise to bring it up to live a good, Christian life.

Catholics and Protestants

Queen Mary I (1553-1558) tried to bring back the Roman Catholic Church, and **executed** over 300 Protestants who refused to give up their new faith. Mary's successor, Elizabeth I, kept the Church of England independent from Rome, supported moderate Protestant reforms, but allowed many Roman Catholic traditions to remain. She ordered everyone to attend church on Sundays, and to worship in the same way. People were fined if they refused.

Protestant churches

By the end of the Tudor era, churches and services had changed greatly. Church walls were whitewashed. Stained glass windows, statues, crosses, candlesticks and incense had been removed, and priests wore plain black robes. There was less music and few processions. Prayers and Bible readings were in English. The priest stood in a pulpit (raised platform) to give sermons (religious lectures), telling people how to behave.

Ideas and Education

The Tudor age was a time of exciting new ideas in science, geography, politics, literature, music, art and design. Most of these ideas came to Britain from abroad.

Some ideas began in Europe, as part of a movement called the Renaissance. They included new artistic styles inspired by ancient Greek and Roman designs, and new medical and scientific knowledge based on ancient Greek discoveries that had been lost for over 1,000 years.

Other new ideas were brought to Britain by explorers who made long, very dangerous voyages overseas. They brought information about distant lands, and described the peoples who lived there. Their reports made Tudor people think about the world in a new, more questioning way.

Read all about it!

All these new ideas were spread by a new technology – printing. This was invented in Germany around 1450. The first printing presses in Britain were set up in 1476 and 1507. They printed religious books, almanacs (lists of important dates and useful information), handbooks on medicine and farming, political pamphlets, music, poems and songs.

◀ The frontispiece (illustrated first page) of *The Mariners Mirrour*, a book full of useful information for sailors, first published in 1579. Like many other rare and valuable early printed books, it is kept in the British Library in London.

A Tudor schoolroom, with two classes. One master, a priest (right) teaches the pupils how to pray. The other master (far left) is listening to pupils reading aloud. He holds a big stick to punish boys who make mistakes.

Education

At the start of the Tudor age, books were mostly read by noblemen and women, merchants and yeomen farmers, because they were the only people who knew how to read and write. Their children were taught at home by their parents, or by private tutors. But during the Tudor period new schools called grammar schools were set up. They had places for any boys whose parents could afford the fees. Schoolmasters taught the boys Latin and ancient Greek as well as how to read and write. Girls did not go to school.

▼ The main courtyard at Magdalene College, part of Cambridge University. Students and their teachers lived and worked here, in study bedrooms with windows looking out over the lawn. Only wealthy men could go to university in Tudor times. A few very rich women – like Queen Elizabeth – employed private tutors to teach them at home. Elizabeth herself was very intelligent and is said to have been able to understand six languages!

The professionals

By the end of the Tudor era there were still only nine British universities, but in Tudor times more places became available for male students. Previously only the rich attended university, but these new students came from merchant families. They later worked in towns – as teachers, lawyers, doctors, writers and priests – living on the fees they received from everyone they served.

War on Land and at Sea

Henry VII, the first Tudor king, came to power in 1485 after a battle at Bosworth Field. That battle was fought by knights in armour charging at each other on horseback, and by foot-soldiers shooting with bows and arrows. Both techniques, however, were becoming old-fashioned.

In Tudor times, there were many new ways of waging war. On land, tube-shaped iron guns brought the biggest changes. They could be huge, like cannons, or small and portable, like hand-held muskets, but they all worked in the same way. Their barrels (tubes) were loaded with an explosive mixture, called gunpowder, plus a solid metal ball. Then the gunpowder was set alight by a smouldering fuse. As it exploded, it shot the ball a long distance with tremendous force.

Cannonballs could smash through stone walls, and crush bodies on a battlefield. The smaller (marble-sized) balls fired by muskets ripped into flesh and shattered bones. Muskets were carried by foot-soldiers. They also fought with pikes (sharp axe blades with spikes, fitted to the ends of long poles).

◀ This reconstruction shows Tudor gunners ready to fire a cannon from a tower at Pendennis Castle in Cornwall. Being a gunner was very dangerous work. Cannons often exploded, killing everyone near by.

In Tudor times, many soldiers were **mercenaries**, who volunteered to fight for anyone who would pay them. This was another big change from earlier periods, when men had been forced to join armies led by their local lord.

Sea battles

There were also major changes in warfare at sea. Before Tudor times, there were no warships. Instead, merchant ships were fitted at the prow (front) and stern (back) with wooden platforms called castles. Soldiers stood there, ready to shoot arrows at enemy ships, or to jump aboard them. Once on deck, they fought using swords.

Henry VIII and the later Tudor monarchs ordered new, purpose-built warships, specially designed for fighting at sea. Each ship was equipped with the latest cannons, and had gun-ports – holes cut in the sides. In a battle, warships sailed as close as they could to the enemy. Then they fired their cannonballs, sinking enemy ships or setting them on fire, and terrorising their crews.

▲ The *Golden Hind* (on the left), the ship of the famous Tudor explorer and pirate Sir Francis Drake (1540-96), attacking a Spanish treasure ship off the coast of South America. You can clearly see the gun-ports in the side of the *Golden Hind*.

▶ Calshott Castle, Hampshire, was one of a series of forts built by Henry VIII to guard the south-east coast of England. That was Britain's closest point to Europe, and all Tudor rulers feared that enemy invaders from France or Spain might try to land there.

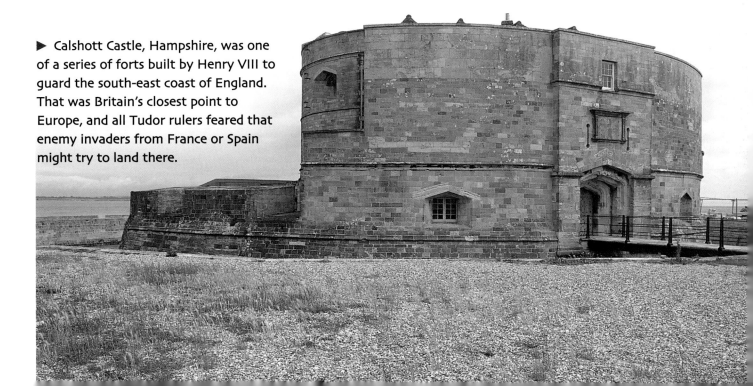

The Tudor Legacy

The long and glorious reign of Queen Elizabeth I came to an end in 1603. In spite of religious quarrels among church leaders, disputes over laws and taxes with Parliament, and threats of invasion from Spain, she had managed to stay on the throne for 45 years.

There was only one royal duty that Elizabeth failed to fulfil. She did not continue the Tudor **dynasty** by having a child. When Elizabeth died, her distant cousin, James Stuart, who was already King James VI of Scotland, became James I of England.

Changing times

The Tudor age saw many changes in Britain. Some led to suffering. Rich people fenced off open land that was once shared by all. Many ordinary people were poor. Some faced hunger and homelessness. Communities struggled to cope as the population increased by almost 50 per cent.

▼ Part of the funeral procession which carried Queen Elizabeth's body to be buried in Westminster Abbey, London, in 1603. All the mourners – and the horses – are dressed in black, as a sign of mourning. This painting is now in the British Library.

▲ The roof of King's College Chapel in Cambridge, built in the reign of Henry VIII, is decorated with carved stone roses – the symbol of the Tudor dynasty. Today, the chapel is visited by millions of people from all round the world.

▼ A comb, some coins, a pocket sundial and a rosary (beads used to help people remember what prayers to say) were all found in the wreck of the *Mary Rose*. Although their owners died almost 500 years ago, the objects have survived until today. Looking at personal items like these can help us understand what Tudor people's lives were like.

But other changes were good. Crafts and trades prospered, towns and cities grew, and nobles, merchants and yeomen farmers all built fine new homes. Tudor armies and navies became stronger. Tudor writers, painters, poets and musicians created great works of art. Tudor rulers encouraged scholarship, exploration and new discoveries.

Surviving from Tudor times

Today we can admire Tudor paintings, furniture, tapestries and jewels in many museums and art galleries, or visit Tudor heritage sites, like the re-built Globe Theatre, or the remains of Henry VIII's warship *Mary Rose*. Tudor buildings also survive in many parts of the country – from grand stately homes and royal palaces to timber-framed cottages and village inns.

Tudor proverbs (popular sayings) are still quoted. 'The love of money is the root of all evil', 'It is more blessed to give than to receive' and 'A multitude of sins' are all quotes from the Tudor translations of the Bible. We also play Tudor music. The tune 'Greensleeves', probably written by King Henry VIII, has become a favourite ringing tone for mobile phones!

Timeline

1485 Henry Tudor defeats King Richard III at the Battle of Bosworth Field and becomes Henry VII.

1487 and **1497** Unsuccessful rebellions against Tudor rule.

1509 Henry VII dies; his son, Henry VIII, becomes king.

1534 Henry VIII becomes head of the Church in England.

1536 England and Wales are united; Beggars Act says all able-bodied beggars should be made to work.

1536-40 Henry VIII dissolves (shuts down) Roman Catholic monasteries and nunneries.

1536-37 People in northern England riot against Protestant religious reforms.

1540s Bad harvests lead to famine in northern and western England.

1547 Henry VIII dies; his son Edward VI becomes king and supports Protestant reforms; Vagrants Act introduces strict punishments for homeless or wandering beggars.

1549 People in East Anglia riot against land enclosures; people in western England riot against Protestant reforms, local landlords, and growing poverty.

1553 Edward VI dies; Mary I, elder daughter of Henry VIII, becomes queen and tries to bring back the Roman Catholic religion.

1558 Mary I dies; her sister, Elizabeth I, becomes queen and compromises over religion.

1577-80 Sir Francis Drake sails around the world.

1588 Spanish Armada (fleet) defeated.

1588 William Shakespeare starts writing plays.

1590s Bad harvests lead to famine in northern and western England.

1598-1601 Parishes are made responsible for helping local poor.

1599 Globe Theatre opens in London.

1603 Elizabeth I dies; Scottish king James VI becomes king of England and Wales.

Places to Visit

Hampton Court Palace, London
Tudor royal palace, with many displays about Tudor life.

Eltham Palace, London
Favourite Tudor royal home.

Tower of London, London
Where many famous Tudor people were imprisoned and executed. It also houses displays of Tudor jewels, weapons and armour.

Globe Theatre, Bankside, London
Reconstructed Tudor theatre where Shakespeare's plays are performed.

Hardwick Hall, Derbyshire
One of the best examples of a Tudor great house, with brick walls and large glass windows.

Stratford upon Avon, Warwickshire
Town with several Tudor buildings and many links with writer William Shakespeare, including the house of his wife, Anne Hathaway.

Royal Dockyards, Portsmouth, Hampshire
Where the remains of Henry VIII's warship *Mary Rose* and objects found on it are preserved.

Kentwell Manor, Suffok
A Tudor house that is now a centre for re-enactments of life in Tudor times.

Dover Castle, Kent
Coastal fort on a cliff, re-built by Henry VIII to defend Britain against invaders.

Lavenham and Kersey, Suffolk
Villages that grew wealthy through the Tudor wool and cloth trade. Many early 16th-century houses remain.

Fountains Abbey and **Rievaulx Abbey, Yorkshire**
Ruins of monasteries shut down by Henry VIII.

Burghley House, Stamford, Lincolnshire
England's largest Tudor stately home, with elaborate stone carvings at the top of its towers.

Glossary

apprentices young men being trained by master craftsmen. An apprenticeship normally lasted for 5 years, and apprentices had to obey strict rules.

bodices the top parts of women's dresses, above the waist.

chandlers people who made and sold candles.

civil war war between people of the same country.

commoners people who were not part of a noble family.

dynasty a succession of rulers of the same family.

executed killed as a punishment.

flax a plant grown for its fibres, which are made into linen.

incense sweet-smelling substances burned to create clouds of perfumed smoke.

Latin the language of the Romans and of the Catholic Church in Tudor times.

mercenaries soldiers who fought for anyone who would pay them.

musket a hand-held gun that fired small metal balls.

nobles people who belonged to families with a title, such as 'duke' or 'lord'.

Parliament meeting of nobles, top priests, and representatives from towns and the countryside. Together, Parliament and the king or queen raised new taxes and passed new laws.

resin a strong-smelling substance found in tree trunks and branches.

tapestries large pictures, woven from coloured silk and wool, and hung on walls.

thatchers skilled workers who made roofs out of dry grass and reeds.

tunic thigh-length outer garment, worn by men.

viols musical instruments with 6 strings, played with a bow.

yeomen wealthy farmers, who owned comfortable houses and large amounts of land.

Books and Websites

Books

Moira Butterfield, *The Diary of an Elizabethan Actor*, Franklin Watts, 2001

Peter Chrisp, *On the Trail of the Tudors in Britain*, Franklin Watts, 1999

Natalie Grice, *The Diary of a Young Tudor Lady-in-Waiting*, Franklin Watts, 2000

Robert Hull, *The Tudors in Their Own Words*, Franklin Watts, 2001

Fiona Macdonald, *You Wouldn't Want to be Married to Henry VIII*, Hodder Wayland, 2001

Elizabeth Newberry, *What Happened Here? Tudor Farmhouse*, A & C Black, 1996

Brian Williams, *Tudor Explorers*, Heinemann, 1993

Rachel Wright, *Craft Topics: The Tudors*, Franklin Watts, 1999

Websites
snaithprimary.eril.net/tudors.htm
Information and activities based on visual evidence from Tudor times.

www.stemnet.nf.ca/CITE/explorer.htm
Site full of information about early European explorers and their voyages to the Americas.

www.tudorgroup.co.uk
Site of an historical re-enactment group with information about life in Tudor times.

www.toweroflondon.com/kids/
Children's guide to the Tower of London, an important Tudor palace.

www. maryrose org./explore
and
www.maryrose.org/lcity
Meet the crew of Henry VIII's warship *Mary Rose*, find out about life on board and the objects recovered from the wreck. For ages 7 to 11.

Index